Petals

ANNA CASAMENTO ARRIGO

PAGE PUBLISHING
Conneaut Lake, PA

First originally published by Page Publishing 2022

ISBN 979-8-88654-807-5 (pbk)
ISBN 979-8-88654-808-2 (digital)

Printed in the United States of America

Dedication

For Dean

Kindness Matters

Foreword

. . . .

I first met Ms. Casamento-Arrigo a couple of years ago on Facebook. I found her an engaging, lively personality, someone who unselfishly helped others, shared their work, and promoted it. In an age of me-my-mine, this is a rare thing. She had suffered through a life-crippling stroke, and she had recovered to not only make it back to the land of the living, but she had also thrived. Her love for life is written into her poetry, and it shows a zest for living as few other poets—in my opinion—can show.

She has shown me—and my guess is, many others—that suffering a physical or mental impairment is not the end of the world. Rather, it is the beginning. Her poems encourage and uplift, and what better testament to life is that? She has been through the proverbial wringer, as it were, experienced the depths of illness and depression, and has emerged stronger than ever.

I have been fortunate enough to have served as a sounding board for her ideas as well as helping her edit her work, and it has been a joy to do so each time. May everyone else be as fortunate to read ***Petals*** and discover the miracle of what life has to offer.

J.S. Frankel

Petals
(with Paul Simeone)

Watching the blooms in early spring
Wondering what else would come calling
Joyfully dancing bare feet under that noon day sun
Holding pocketful of dreams and things undone
And autumn too quickly filters in
Announcing in grandiose and flair with that not so gentle wind

Petals one by one floating lazily beneath the wary sun
Where time wishes for those things undone

And winter blared with icy bits of this and then
Time so little left before snow ushered in—
Petals some as the day earth recalled
Waltzed along my bare toes unfurled

Petals one by one floating beneath the wary sun
Where time wishes for those things undone

And I—a final La Jota Moncadena petals and me
Catch. Release. Step upon the tide of the torrent sea

One two three taken into time's embrace
Journey after journey no fear of time no fear of space

Petals one by one floating beneath the wary sun
Petals. Just petals and I as one.

(Song version on YouTube @annacasamentoarrigo)

1

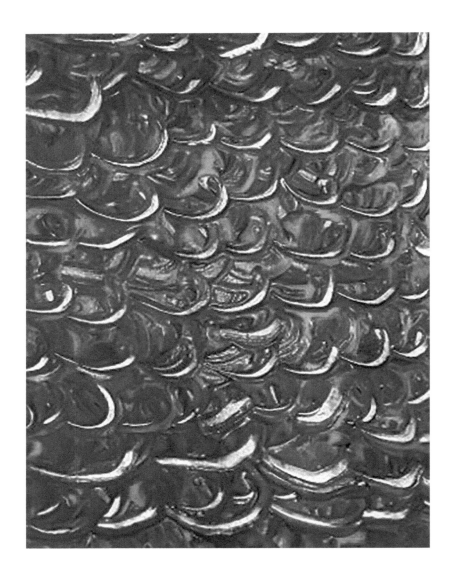

The Perfect Distance

(By ACA and Paul Simeone-song on
YouTube @annacasamentoarrigo)

I watch as they kneel to pray
Thinking of the words I can no longer say
And in the perfect distance I—unseen
Wondering, why did you have to be so mean?
The perfect smile upon your face and I
Living in the shadow of a lie…

Where does a devil sleep?
With the secrets he will keep…

Why did you do that to me?
Why did you do that to me?

Do hear my voice so small
Pleading out and Ohhhhhhh
Taking my breath—watching me fall
Pleading out and Ohhhhhhh

Where does a devil sleep?
With the secrets he will keep.

While Mom waits restless by the phone
And Dad travels far from home.
And the world questions why
Once believing the shadows and the lie—

I watch as they kneel to pray
With angel wings my dad just made—

3

Why did you do that to me?
Why did you do that to me?

Ended my hopes, dreams, and all—
Taking my breath—watching me fall?

Where does this devil sleep?
With the secrets he will keep.

Why did you do that to me?
Why did you do that to me?

Slaying Windmills

Slaying Windmills
Time the enemy
Lurking in the shadows
Or is it fretfully tossing about
In the yonder fallow field—
Where Sancho holds court
Rocinante king
Did you forget?
Don't you know…
Slaying Windmills
(Foiled-Forlorn-Foolish Don—
(Fearing-Faithful-Failing… Famed Infamy)
So many Windmills left unclaimed…
You would do well to listen…

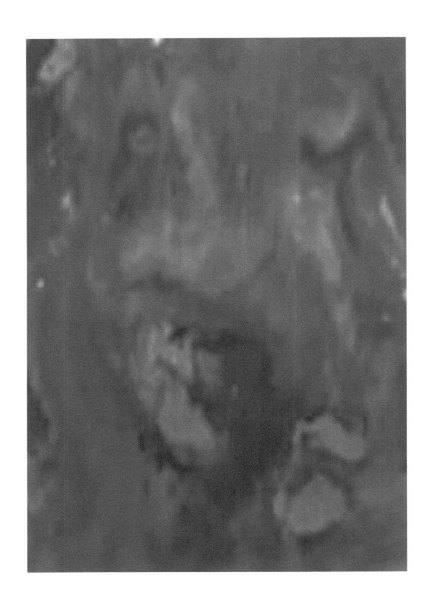

"BUTTERFLIES AND BUMBLEBEES"

• •

(ACA and Paul Simeone-Song on YouTube @annacasamentoarrigo)

My spirit rises and falls
Upon the foam of the evening tide
And joyfully welcomes the summer sun
And I close my eyes

The happy yellow warmth
Dances in seductive playfulness
Behind my eyelids, the ocean's song
Ebbs and flows
The song ebbs and flows

(CHORUS)
Watching butterflies and bumblebees
Butterflies and bumblebees
Rising, floating, laughter, joy
Content to be…no more
No less, no more

My mother's lullaby
Filling me again
And then again with an urgency
Too mighty to repress

I am alive once more
My youthful fancies free
My senses heightened, tingling
Like the kiss of an evening breeze
An early evening breeze

(CHORUS)

Silence Speaks

In silence
blissfully capturing my dreams
In bare feet the squish-squish-squish
Wherever I care to slip and glide
And Mother Earth knows me well…
With those wispy winds
Tenderly she smooths away all else…
As is her want—
Silence
Hitching a welcome flight upon autumn's amber
Listen
Silence Speaks!

An Adventure

Alone not lonely
Meandering down one path
Magical
Majestic
Invincible
Knights and Paupers
Dining with Kings
The unexpected
An image in the distance
Many images
Swallowing my breaths
A twist
Foreshadowing
In labyrinthine swirls
Transfixed
Turning
Turning
Weaving magical
Spells

Voce Forte

I questioned the journey
My steps…tenuous…
My mind in soothing words
White feathers
And lemon tea kisses
Licking away yesterday's fears…
And
Only then
did my words
in voce forte
Broke free and I
Sang in the early morning rain
Forging beyond…ignoring
That bothersome Mephistopheles
Screeching in protest
'If tomorrow starts without me'
'If tomorrow starts with ME!'
Freedom…

Hey! Child

Hey! Child, are you happy in this wondrous world,
Or are you dreaming of something more?
Have you greeted the summer wind
Danced between raindrops in spring?
Hey! Child are you finding beauty in the unseen
And gathering memories of the places you've been?
Hey! Child are you—?

Twilight

Fading
Falling
Feeling the surf's rush
Fast and furious
Fantastically
Fearlessly
Floating
Farther and farther
Far into the forever
Finding
Freedom
In tender moments
When you took me in your arms
Caressed my spirit
With your heart
Before twilight
Chorused
Our Forever—

More than Now

● ●

Long into the night
My breath in whispers—
A greeting
Star bursts and the moon retreats
Lifting the sleepy veil whereupon the celestial slumber
And in contentment's waking…
Take my hand
Come!

Your Surf's Song

Fast and furious floating upon the ebb and I
In joyous rhythm
My sleepy soul
Waking
My heart in carefree splashing
Tiptoeing
Hoarding the remnants of the evening tide
Holding on
Letting go
Come—
Dance
Your surf's song
—and you?

17

Canceling the Breech

Raise up your wall entombing the shadows
Sucking in the finality that birthing…breech
Agony muffledcrushedcancelledfreedom…pull the alarm
And sit back—
Lie back—
Peer out from the rose glasses and…do what you will
While the maddeningdeafening screeches (in
protests and misguidedjudgments)
Canceling the Breech
And canons drone out convictions
Affirming a righteous hit—
Canceling the Breech—
Peering over that invisible wall
Masses—
Praying
Hallelujah
And herded overunderbetweenbesidebeyond
The blaring sirensandhope
Recalling days of empty—
A void and it goesandcomes upon the rhetoric
of…to the leftrightleftrightleftright
We're the canceledbreech
Wading the calm of tides
Knowing tomorrow's bombsburstingmidair
and seven is notjust another number
Nortenthirteen
Falllaygiveback
Calling gatherers and hoarders
To breach
Humm
The parade awaits your arrival
Downupupupup

18

From NewYorktoCaliforniatoAlaskatoHawaiitotheretoo
Your doctor is on call donning threemasksvaxcard—
He draws out his measuring tape and his government
approved mechanical hand teetering
At the end of a sixfootpole
Canceling the Breech
Canceling the Breech—
Listening to a private Hallelujah!

.

My Waltz

Touching my senses
With a stinging in my veins
Holding me
Drowning me
My body
My soul (pure and whole) followed
Ah!
Flying back up to the sky—
Holding that memory
And the echoes of that last verse...refrain
My forever waltz among the stars.

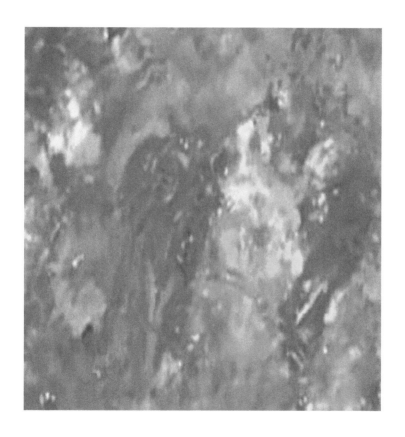

Watch Me Now!

• •

There was no time for the brutalized
To rise in righteousness indignation
(Who would care even if they had)?
A stifling of those wants
Hope
Dreams
Gave way
The parting of…the Sea
Foam caressing white sands—
And history—
Snickered
Well?
Watch me…
Now!

Treading

So long ago
And yesterday's songs
Not far from the now
When childhood dreams
Marched in
One by one
Brandishing laurels of possibilities
Probabilities
And Dreams...again
And again.
I had so many steps untraveled
And, in my mind, nothing
No one would question
Which road I'd take
But adulthood's arrival
Acrimonious
Contentious
Daring me
Urging me to tread along
Trampling Dreams
My will gave way
To an unfamiliar knock upon my door
My mind...imploded
And just like that
The then
When aspirations
Exciting
Beckoning
Welcoming a new tomorrow
Fell away.
A new, but now familiar dirge wafts in
And the stench hails down

Like a cataclysmic mud slide
And I
Chase away demons
With happy pills
(That never make me happy, truth be told)
Nursing the remains of last night's cheer—
Ominously glaring in the early dawn
There...
Marching in place
Grey Goose
Taunting me again
While Johnny Walker burdened with Four Roses
And wearing a Crown Royal
Treading
Treading
Sunsets
Giving way to the blurred-out moon
And tenuous stars...
Ennui sets in
And I so yearn for yesterday's possibilities and dreams
Treading
Treading
To Tuesdays and Thursdays
Begging for alms
Under a street light
And dreams
Of possibilities!

The Comeback Warrior

Call
-kcab
Come
-kcab
Touch
-kcab
Full
-kcab
Half
-kcab
Hold
-kcab
Take
-kcab
Shrink
-kcab
Keep
-kcab
Date
-kcab
Think
-kcab
Pay
-kcab
Set
-kcab
Backdrop…
Fight *Back!*

Bubbles

While tiny hands
Dare to gather silky threads
In the distance
Butterflies and bumblebees
Hitch transitory rides upon
Bubbles and memories
While the sun sets
And stars gather
Upon the forever
Of many wheres and whens
Remembering bubbles and sunsets.

The Missing Pieces

∙∙

-& years from now
when the disquiet & chaos
subsides
& Dawn breaks through
that veil of contentions
misdirections
& the masses
like that puzzle
(The one with so many missing pieces)
still…
served a greater purpose
& The lost & found
fill the voids
peace

Finally... Silence

Finally…as the last resounding shattering
(Screeching out in protest)
Of that watchtower clock
(Whose face too long had met torrential rain and forlorn nights—
and whose hands had lost
The most rudimentary task-infinite seconds and…)
Silence!
Woebegone…
Aching
…and stagnant anticipation…
Finally…who will keep those dashes
The between Time?
Birth-Death…
Silence!
Finally…dawn arrives purring
Paws
In their fuzzy fluidity and Finally…
That ear piercing… Silence!
Did it awaken you?

Child of Loneliness

What persistent memories lay hidden
just behind those violet eyes?
And hold your dreams captive
In that transient peace but, in reality, (in torment) beg...release?
Child of Loneliness?
Has your mind (composed and playfully imagining
the feel of snowflakes upon your tongue)
Ever seen beauty through your heart?
What words have yet to journey past
Those rosebud lips
And, in one glorious sunburst—
Trumpet out your world?
Child of Loneliness?
Have you heard the chorus song of the Passerine at daybreak
In each summer's wind?
And in that unfettered burst of hope (the one you've yet to share)
danced!

Life Speaks Loudly!

And with the Springs' warmth
(The sad, lonely branch long removed)
A gentle crackling
almost imperceptible at first—
Did louder grow
& There
Yes, there
Where the sad & lonely branch had been felled in an icy storm
Just last winter(you see)
Left reminders of what would be—
Life!

The Beguiling

. . . .

Trailer on YouTube.
Narrated by Marnye Young and Lucas Webley.

Shall I find your eyes
Piercing that opaque facade
And with the gentleness of your fingertips
tug, pull, shred away suppression
In a humbling pang of longing—
Look into the night
And free those desires
So long untended?
Shall I find your lips
Soft against each part of me
Warming the frigid winter's chill?
Shall I—
not in the before or after
Find you…carrying my breaths and sighs
Catch my happy tears
In your heart
And hold them
For eternity?
Shall I call your name at dawn
When orgasmic beauty fades
And still—
Find you here?

My Naked Soul

Inhale
Exhale
Each breath
Warm against my own skin
And where the endlessly soothing
Ebb and tide
Meet the horizon
And Mother Earth
Calls forth with her lush and familiar cadence
Heaven's gate
Listening
There
Not beforeafternow
My Naked Soul
And…
Come Andromeda
Let's dance!

Truth and Illusions All

Shhhh…no one knows I'm here—
Suspended above
A field
Snapdragons
Shhhh…no one knows I'm here—
Breathing in illusion
Exhaling
Deeply
Exhaling
Truth…
Shhhh…no one knows I'm here.

Home

• •

Home—
Beyond a path
Whereupon thistles are found
And their journey fickle
As a summer's wind
Converging
Diverging
Lifting
Dropping
Lifting
Dropping
Home—
Beyond
Where that path
Where even my shadow
(Once followed…but, now)
Journeys
Lifting
Dropping
Diverging
Searching
Chasing
The fickle summer's wind
Too long caught in the failing
Falling far behind
Fearing
Where once there was no fear
As the dancing branches of that scraggly old and failing magnolia
Did master fantastic terrors
Chameleonesque
Scratching at the window
Pain—

With both impunity
And orchestrated control
In shadows—my mind
Transforms those sickly branches
Commanding
The innocent
Fragile be those shadows   ·

And they're forever
Etched upon the walls of my home
Where I, in my mind (my shadow leading the way)
Shall in a shattered disquiet
Find
What I had always known
Home.

Time

∙ ∙

And in time—
When home fell off horizon's amber and…
Oh! That ethereal hint of what, I assume—
Heaven.
I held close memories
One by one
Melting
Under a buttery sunrise…
My forever time.

Who Am I?

I am my nonna
With papyrus fingers
Embroidering flowers
Along the blue velvet hem
Of my skirt
And at five
Sitting on the creaking floorboards
Peering up
The scent of nonna's bread
Wafting from that brick oven
Mingling with the fresh figs
Whose aroma lingered in the air
And cradled me in the familiar…
I am my mama
Collecting cherries from the orchard
Our fingers in hues of red and…
Sunshine
Dancing to music no one else could hear
And watching
It was enough
In the then—
And sitting at her feet
Warming my tiny frame
Cinnamon
Bay leaves
And lavender
Floating from the pot in the fireplace
Listening
As mama wove fantastic tales of kings
Queens
And happily ever afters—
Who Am I?

The Hoarder of Dreams

· ·

Here he goes again…
And again—
The Hoarder of Dreams—
Double-tongued…slurping a few
While those razor talons
(Having trampled each flicker under a moonless sky)
Shreds the remainders…
He's not Mephistopheles…
I wonder—nonetheless.

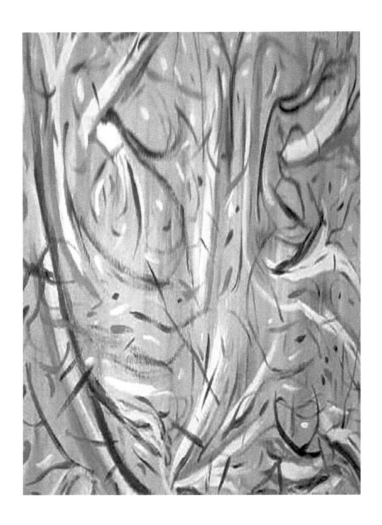

A Slow Dance in the Summer Rain

Author's narration on YouTube and TikTok.

What pleasure we found—scooped up and
tucked it all away in our memory trove
And…
Listening to the music of our early pleasures…youth
Before we thought our elders were…
And having common sense to come in out
of that summer thunderstorm—
Remember the one that had me sheltered in your beach body arms
As the joyful downpour somehow
Made our passionate kisses fuller…deeper…and for that
moment as the silk sand became our birthing…ah!
Foundations.
Before the creases mocked that long ago
And holding hands became our all—
And tomorrow…tomorrow
A Slow Dance in the Summer Rain
And that old, frayed plaid shirt (the one that
always smelled of car oil and hard work)
Such silly disagreements…and now
When I feel the now slipping away
I wear that old, frayed plaid shirt
Remembering
A Slow Dance in the Summer Rain
And the safety of your arms…
Still.

Nonno's Orchard

5-year-old bare feet
follow my nonno
Down the cliffs
Push at an ancient gate
welcome heaven
Blueberries
Crunched squirt
Sweet nectar
It was their welcome
Boysenberries, mulberries higher up on
Massive bushes
Growing old and tired
Gave easily to my eager hands
Nonno smiled.
Yellow galoshes covered with dried mud.
Walking home the squish-squish of the water
Squish-squish as each step brought you closer
Squish-squish
As your now wet socks
Squish-squished along
Gosh! I wish I still had those yellow galoshes!

Laughter

By the age of 8
All I knew of life—
Death
Spirit
Dreams
Trust
Angels will not
Fly
With broken wings
then
There you were
Stilled manicured
Fingers
Resting
Upon that tweed suit
You hated so very much
Pink lips
And all
Your eyes glued
Shut
12
Thought I heard your laughter.

In Devi's Love

I have tasted of the earth
Traveling long
Wandering far
Gliding upon gossamer wings
Floating
Gently
Deftly
My breaths and sighs
In serene repose
Content.
To feast upon both air and sky
And in Devi's hands
My joy abounds
And whispers in the tenderness
Beyond the stars.

Holding on Letting go

It hadn't been an easy death
But the will to die was less than my will…to survive
The stench of torn flesh
Gathered in haphazard mounds upon the floor
And (I felt no pain, indeed)
Fillets and pounds of flesh
Commingling with the smell of metal
(And I found myself comforted by that)
From the unseen
Lying beneath my covering
(The one apportioned to both man and
beast and creatures in between)
Long into the night
Until my body
Or that temporary facade monikered mortality
Became lighter
And during the during
I fancied the serenity
Of a time, when a chasm fashioned in lilies,
tulips, and a single yellow rose
And those, now cement walls caked in splatters of the blood letting
Would implode and a return to earth in newfound darkness
Holding on
Letting go
A separation
Decisive
And in eternities bound…
Where my projected self-free falls
Letting go
And in those moments of the nano seconds before
Where my psyche severed ties with real
Time…

A zither and tabla with its stretched goat skin…(and
I wondered if it had let go during the during)
In tempo still, beyond my musings
A chant fixed
In a trance
Letting go
Holding on…
And, just like that
I was renewed
As if inexplicably awakened from a night terror
Where
horrors
Painfully disturbing
Your body your soul
Swept up and the unseen evils of the unreal
Enslave your mind
Ravage your facade
Puppeteer your will
And grind (or try to) the remnants of your psyche and spirit
And so it is…
As the swells of both zither and tabla
In unison
Lift the heavens…
Come
Listen
Om Namah Shivaya
My inner self
Holding on!

Devils take the Hindmost

Scampering about
feet shuffling in boots he'd fished out of that dumpster
Not long ago…
Like so many-agape-bellowing out(for those who
hear—welcome one and welcome all)
From one alley to the next—
On good days, imported tenderloin with a smattering of—
Au jus and a side…white asparagus today (Sweet Pea
Chef—would have preferred to serve Hop Shoots from
Behar had the bourgeois, with their invisible halos
and condescending orders…never mind…)
And dumpster diving, the growing sport as 'those'—you know, the
ones you cross the street to avoid that familiar stench of poverty
And so…
The discarded, yesterday's reminders of those manicured
fingers wearing their mere facades of life
In marbled hallways and a white-gloved hand
behind imported this and that—
Scampering in their designer shoes whose echo bounces
off their Michael Arman tortoise shell…
Perhaps, accumulating a wealth of knowledge…
Ah! What a methodical journey and forever
The accumulation of that coveted treasure of knowledge—
Have you found your strength
And sought beyond acquisitions, where
determination is your illusion's realm?
Understanding that that great divide isn't so great after all—
Devils take the Hindmost.

Love Lives in the forever

in angelic whispers
the ethereal
ray
summons
the slumbering soul
hold fast
sweet innocence
it sings
a voce dolce
piano
piano
walking
on air
deeper
deeper
where forest
meets meadow
sleep
while in crystal drops
alight
to gather
star dust
creating a golden path
…where love—
Here—
There…
Lives on!

Embracing—
The forever as
night
F
A
L
L
S
sleeps
the soul—
Only to awaken comfortably resting in his mother's forever.

Autumn Whispers

· ·

Autumn whispering her entrance

And eagerly I follow

(As I have so many times before)

My spirit guiding my steps

And in the now, dawn begins anew…

Butterflies and Bumblebees

• •

Author's song with music and vocals by
Paul Simeone found on Youtube.

(Original Poem—ACA)

My spirit rises and falls
Upon the foam of the evening tide
And joyfully welcomes the summer sun
And
I close my eyes
As
The happy yellow warmth
Dances in seductive playfulness
Behind my eyelids
The ocean's song
Ebbs and flows
…my mother's lullaby
Filling me again
And then again with an urgency too powerful
To repress…
Alive once more
My youthful fancies
Like that first bite into a juicy plum
My senses tingling…heightened
Watching butterflies and bumblebees
Rising
Floating
Laughter
Joy

Content to be…
No more
No less—
Oh! Tender the kiss of an early evening breeze
That found me
Watching butterflies and bumblebees!

The Maddening

Reaching up
Piercing through those nebulous clouds
Grasping the first
—as nighttime
Etched upon the pallet
In infinite hues
Yet to be named—
Stillness
Welcoming the fragile soul
Which decades hence played fisticuffs
With the heavens
Far
So far beneath that happy hunting ground—
Rejoicing as the summer rain
A seductive dance
Somewhere between…upon that Utopian rainbow
A dance whispers through…
A Bachata and Zouk—
Rising
My souls
Alive once more (each different…diverse—yet the same)
Merrily respond—
Watch me Now!

The Magician

. . . .

It is here
Beneath a moonless sky
Where those primal urges
Too long suspended
Repressed
Suppressed
Untended
And…in anticipation
Muttering
Yet…
Dare I invite you into my night
Beneath that moonless sky
A woman and a man
Unearthing…exploring…discovering
The Magician's sleight of hand—
Illusions given away
Where awareness and truth
Reign
In the realm of love's domain—
Ah!

The Weight of Shadows

Cloaked in yesteryear's
Of the lost
Forgotten
Found
In the unlatching of that treasure trove
Impatiently waiting your return
Piercing the cobwebs' strands
Howling your name
Prompting your return
In disquiet
Breaking
Sifting
Through moments caught in that Hasselblad
Frayed
In muted hues of golden wheat
Piled
Lovingly secured with lace
And sun-kissed bouquets of wildflowers
The Weighted Shadows
And nudging
Your papyrus hands
Caught in that aria—
And soaring well beyond those moments
Where
Decades ago
And seconds
Ago—
Mortality…
Lighter—
Pure—
Simpler—
Dared you on…

In the then
You responded
And The Weight of Shadows…
Mephistopheles
Was lost and gone
Lost and gone.

Hollow Men

Come meet, if you dare, the Hollow Men
Gathering, one and all, momentum
Their coffers overflowing with idle gossip
Centuries old—
Eating away that sunshine…
Fueled by those (who, with ceaseless impunity
and unrest, still dare to dream)
Raging flames…
Peering through…angry wisps
Of grey smoke—
Scooping out bits of bone—
There
just out of Anubis' reach…
Rejoicing—
Ears perched…
Hearing that cacophonous yelping of the Bargest—
Come meet, if you dare, the Hollow Men
Let the damned and cursed night
Guide your steps…
Look not to ease your weary mind—
Too long in shadows and—
Listening to the long gone tune of thy lyre—
Release the black birds
Your crows
Ravens
Vultures too long gorging on your thoughts
Set free the monarch…butterflies and candles
Past Hypos…hesitate no longer…
Come meet, if you dare, the Hollow Men!

A Poet's Soul

Today I shall listen to that voice
Which tortures me
Haunts my dreams
Holds captive that which yearns for freedom
Lost and found
Lost and found—
Purring…
Signaling…in soft secretive undertones
Only I can hear…
And in that moment
(When my soul sighs in susurration and hums)
My soul awakens
To those musings just beneath—
And in that monumental moment
My soul soars once more
Burrowing…out the hint of a voice
And awakening that poet's soul…
Feel it…sense it…
What pain is this?
What ignoble muse lies secretly between the lines
And every word?
What beauty will you find beneath the
grotesque—the maimed—and bruised?
Between the words…will you find your senses heightened?
And peer into this poet's Soul?

Wrapped in Your Heart

Of all that is seen
And yet to be seen
Or not at all
In disquiet and sleeplessness
When unwelcome specters
Awaken me
In cacophonous jeers and taunts
From somewhere
Lying still in sweet repose
In the forever
Your domain
Kingdom
Festooned in all things utopian
Tranquil
And cherubs caress their golden harps
Softly
Deftly
Chasing away ghosts…
And the evils lurking on hell's threshold
You and only You
Hear the teardrops
In those moments of terror
Uncertainty
Fear
It is…
You
Scooping me up
With reminders of the sun
Soon to rise
And only when You
Wrap me in your heart—
I nuzzle at your neck

My breath
Your breath
In unison
A violin sonata
Pulsating from Your soul to mine
And my spirit…halcyon
A lullaby and candy Dreams
Finding me
Wrapped in Your Heart

Follow me!

Follow me beyond the shadow's realm
Tightly hold my hand
I shall guide you far into that magical domain
Where the stars shine brightest
And the shadow swallowed by that forever
That blind faith and your heart
Our hearts…one beat in floating…pulsating
And inch by inch in tempo to those ethereal nights
Far beneath…
Perseus' arms guarding those…
Unearthing of desire…
And—
Make jealous even those constellations
Whose existence (caught in time and astral mystery of beginnings)
Will breathe in those fleeting moments
Of one beauty
One heartbeat…
Follow me!

Guises and Mis...directions

He spoke of Shakespeare and Poe—
And I welcomed such eloquence...
Caught in those moments when the world
Drifted away
Laughing as he entertained me
With barbs and trivia
I so appreciated that reprieve
Alas, such betrayals, guises, and mis...directions
Under the star-embroidered cape
Where the truth...a magician's sleight of hand—
I had ignored...unquestioningly
Caught in that widow spider's web (hiding—
unfazed by the impending thunderstorm)
And a phantasm's stare into my heart—
Surrendering...blindly...gave my mind
Fell hard
Hitting my fragile-naïveté belief
Shakespeare and Poe
Comparing...in Search of Eldorado
While reviling-misdirected my thoughts
The truth...a lie
Penning words that captured falling stars—
In guise and mis...directions...
Lands the broken heart
Disrobing my naïveté
Left bare
My mind...my mind
Trembling—my heart and soul
Truth
In guises and mis...directions!

Awakening Shadows

Where my heart leads
My mind may follow…
The sun's reflection
Casting bursts upon that ancient
Dial…
Time…
Time and the turning…
Spring—
Summer—
And in the mask of autumn ambers…
A social path—
A melting of thoughts—
As Father Frost
Thaws out that dormant psychopath
He's been so cold for so long
In the shadow of mind…

Petals 2

I had not dared looked behind
My heart knew better
Then to dismiss the beauty beneath
Strung on autumn's bare branches
…carry on
…move on
…listen to the call of that which fills those voids…
Your heart will know…
Let those rhythms
Lift your guarded steps…
Too long—heavily clunking
Echoing in the dark
Relentless…menacing
Under a moonless night
Such feeble attempts…
Broken faith…
Parched
Shriveled
Desiccated…wisdom arose
As I…in that beauty
My heart still listening
Allenge and
Pas de bourse…
Scooping petal dustings
The heart knows!

The often-forgotten Working Class Hero

• •

Year after year, grandpa
Tilling the Earth
calloused hands—his victory scars
Sometimes, he'd sit
looking to that seventh heaven
as gentler times floated in on the west wind
in measured movements (none wasted)
his fingers would play with the soil
speaking words of comfort
inspiration
perseverance
hope
as each evening (just before sunset)
He whispered words, like a lullaby
only Mother could hear

Waitin'
sittin'
'kneelin'
prayin'
when buds would bloom!

Metal & Vodka

Behind the locked door
That once filled bottle (Vodka—that magical
elixir to heaven's guarded gate)
Pungent aromas lingering in the mid-morning chill
Open windows and swaying curtains
Catching the remainders—Grey Goose
And carrying them toward the sky
Where the rise and fall
An unwelcoming dance—
Sifting through the pain…as if
Where moments just before catatonia
Set in the scarlet metallic enticing urge
Begged for deeper cuts
Her pain so deep
Her soul had died
As with each thrust and slash
Of an overused box cutter
Without precision
Broke away the flesh…
Her soul had died long ago, after all.
Have you caught its aura floating
To that seventh heaven?
Her vision blurred
Heightened
Then
Dropping
The sweetest offering
Metallic in varying hues of scarlet and crimson
Her treasured…final call
From just beyond
And in that psychotic…anguish
She lay still…silent

72

A crimson blanket of metal and vodka
And days would come and go
While her body prone
Arms and legs cuffed
To that newly sanitized hospital bed—
Awakened
Sleeping child of rumination and surrender
Your Metal and Vodka will be there
Holding captive your soul!
I had not cut deeply enough
More vodka…perhaps
Wishing no pain on those who cared
But, quite simply, needing to end my own!

Puppet Master

Too long silence followed my wayward steps
Listening to a woodpecker
Pecking in cacophonous rhythm
The barren limb of a once majestic
Ancient
Llangernyw Yew
Felled by the ravenous blizzard
The very same one
That covered city sins
As toddlers—noses pressed against shoddy window
Panes
Dreamed of snow angels
And daddy's coming home…
Dressed in those comforter (though they weren't very comforting)
Venturing out…anchored in red made-for-toddler sleighs…
Lost in the whiteout of it all
We didn't mind the constant burst of prestige crystalline treasures
(Our eyes tightly sealed while, in eager anticipation—
our mittened hands—grandma's last Christmas
offering-outstretched-such the Puppet Master…)
From that place where (some believe) orchestrates such majesty—
Down one hill…daddy steering
As I struggled, with mittened hands simultaneously
catching snowflakes and crystals upon my eager tongue
Daddy's frayed cloak—warmth…
my salvation!

Whilst I Escape

· ·

it is that hidden magic
tightly held and guarded
were I to awaken
unmasked
my fleshscape
aroused
preceding
that intimacy…
the first taste…circling upon an axis—
whilst Shiva and Parvati
in desire
immobilized
their gaze transfixed
upon the fleshscape
mesmerized
there…beneath those stars
where The Herdsman and his Weaver
Girl cling onto their eternity—
stars pale

and I…

suckling the remnants of passion fruit
from your fingertips.

Sounds and Silent Seas

· ·

you gave me your music
In rise and runs
Ecstasy joins
passion
Chasing away some wasted tears
Still waiting for the fog
To lift—
Chasing shadows in the night………
Are you there?
Lying still
Your voice—silenced
Where no sound should be
Forming singular bubbles beneath the untraveled sea
Yet, I hear you!
Your words soft…gentle…warm
In mind…in my mind… I hear you. I hear you!
Caresses
Gentle
Tender
My awakening
Once more in anticipation and longing…waits…revisits
…take me—wherever you may go
let the sun, who's setting—disrobed—
finds us
It too has waited our return
When music
Keeps tempo
With our silence…
Are you there?

When Words Run Dry

I fear our liberties trampled
and hacked by blades
piercing the night
Silencing my voice… Words are death—
and
She fears the hate
beguiled
camouflaged
fueled by…what
Some
deem a societal plague
of Revolutionaries
whose time to die
comes too late
strip away the last of my pleasures
Thoughts
Opinions transformed
crystals scooped up
thrown down into that great abyss
farther
deeper
through the dungeons of Hell
Never mind.
We're here!

Nothing More

∙∙∙∙∙∙∙∙∙∙∙∙∙∙∙∙∙∙∙∙∙∙∙∙∙∙∙∙∙∙∙∙∙∙∙∙∙∙∙

sun scorched
so too will the moon
under a hazy heaven
trembling above
in rum-soaked burlap
hues
peel away the mask you wear
and
reveal thy soul's Truth
This
and
nothing
More!

The Gatekeeper

Kneel, you insolent fool
Your games of pretend are at the end
Strutting in your peacock feathers
Pendants…chains…your gold pocket watch
Do not impress the gatekeeper
Standing at the threshold
Your arrangements fated.
How could you not know you did not know?
You who belongs to no one
Least of all yourself—
How could you not know you did not know?
The gatekeeper had been standing in wait
Amusing himself with the daily reports
of your gains and losses
That which had you strutting—
Thumbing your nose
you and your penguin suit—
That which left you kneeling
agonizing the loves lost.
How could you not know, you did not know?
Your room awaits.

Set the Alarm

There are gargoyles afoot
Some rolling in on evening tides
Razor talons sifting pink sand as they go—
Some swooping down in packs
in darkness
Feasting on chaos and causticity.
Some from beneath the shifting plates
with magma orbs
But
All living upon the stench of hate.
Gratified
they trample (some with horny toes) the remnants
of a cornucopia…of malcontents…rich…poor…young…old…
yeah…those
too.
Chuckling (as Gargoyles do) at the Rip Van Winkles
who stretch, yawn, and roll over—
Sleeping till the alarm, they never set, wakes them.

The Reality

Where does your reality reign?
Does it free-float the parallel-Utopia?
Or hold private conference with Medusa—
(Beautiful daughter
sitting by the seas
her wings unconstrained
Primping her hair
Arranging the strands with nimble fingers
Like silky bronze strands of yesterdays
dangling from the queen's neck)
Immune to the fanged attempts
by Her, sometimes, impish snakes?
Has your heart turned to stone?
Where does your reality reign?
Talking history with evil icons
that time does alter for a greater good
(perhaps because they had reminded us of ourselves)?
Where does your reality reign?
Do you speak with Plato? Socrates? Aristotle? Pythagoras?
Have you discovered (through this philosophical
discourse) the rationale for your reality?
Have you gained a broader sense (why are we born)—
knowledge—the reality of their truth)?
Where does your reality reign?
Sipping sweet wine (with greedy haste…one anxious gulp)
Circe watching your piggishness inhale this and that…
In your reality had you noticed that bejeweled wand
(so comfortable, welcomed, and satiated
were you—shared your reality…?)
Forever a pig
Where does your reality reign?

The Vortex

Beyond those tumbles
My arms outstretched
The spirited sun
In mischievous barbs
Passing mockingly above the throbbing
ache...my mind
Adorning my head
The Medieval Maiden
In golden hues of mocking possibilities
Probabilities...
The truth
Swatting away my youthful...naivete
Fickle fantasies of golden headdresses
Passing over
Under
My neck
Extending
In Arms and
Armor
Nobly I dance
upon the barbed wire—
...in the Vortex
where I always welcomed the parade of jesters
—my innocence—
Aching for... Angel lutestrings
And laurel crowns
fashioned by that spirited sun
The Vortex...and I
unhooked
Possibilities...extending far
Beyond
Above
Freedom
...and my childhood naivete.

Born at Sunset

Where lies the sunset
for far too long I've lain
Caught in that state—
before the budding seedling bursts into bloom—
and dormant beneath a blanket…soft vermillion sky
In the fantastic yearnings for My Renaissance—
Or still
within reminiscences of possibilities and
Seated upon the throne
born of Middle Ages and Stone
or star gazing under a periwinkle sky,
Up upon my paladin's shoulders
My master swordsman…
has taught me well—
Reaching
Reaching
the Apex
Wishing I had been born
before Sunset!

Ode to Hendrix

One mind
One Soul
Riding the waves to hell
My night music
The once murmuring flickers
Now consumed
Vibrating
Gyrating
Familiar
in the 60's of my spirit
Hendrix
caressing-attacking-one-two-three
Tunes
Rising…
Fender Stratocaster…white
that lingers—
—burn—hell—burn!

The Red Knight

Come!
Though the ominous shadows
Cast down to the trampled ground
Where that once pious knight
garbed in scarlet red armor
awaits in darkness
calling from the recesses beneath a hallowed moon
—and there
The Corinthian Mountains do well to listen to
the baying of the wolves
bellowing out
Such raucous
Caterwauling
In packs…
Dare not glance behind
for fear has left its tangible markings
in blood and stone…
A long-ago wretched…betrayal
his heart upon that spear-centuries gone—
OH!
Where mortals
Once impaled upon that very same valiant spear
Blessed with holy water by unholy hands,
lift up their eyes
but
Not their hearts
and in voluminous utterings
Spewing out, "God's will'
The Red Knight
in unfathomable anguish and grief
Calls out the demons…
His sword fever charged

slashing
piercing
agape that mortal wound
once a testament to all the pious pretenders
and in that solitary thrust
crimson
The Red Knight—Transylvania
not so long ago…
and darkness calls…announcing
In that Dragon's breath
Dracula!

Fire!

· ·

and where his lips landed
Fire…
consuming
maddening
We inhaled each other's tenderness—
lingering
filling those nooks and crevices
No longer aching—
Fire!
-and holding on—
Fire!
at last…

my blood begins to boil—
…your taste—
My forever

Fire!

She will NOT yield

Sitting back
Mamma catches her breath
though those whimsical winds test her strength
Yielding is never an option
Her aria dulce
piano
forte
humming along
Testing that warrior always—
always in fierce defiance through tempests fierce
She will *NOT* yield!

My Tomorrow's Song

Long gone that wilderness

Collecting flora

A queen's crown

and loneliness

lay dormant just beyond

in isolation

weaving suppression

glaring in envy

hate

its compensation

insult and injury

Solitarily it will thrive

in that self-imposed isolation

Ennui

and I

once child of that glorious

Wilderness

Dressed regally

Shall softly humm

My tomorrow's song

Come!

A Woman's Smile

• •

And as he cradled her body
those repugnant demons recoiled
with a cantankerous thud
fading-fading-fading
—it was just then
her smile caressed her lips
and it was in the tell-tale lapse
just beyond
within
her melancholy gaze
he realized…wondered
what secrets lay in those restless nights
whereupon she sought his touch
that tenderness
forever constant
yielding…yielding
nothing more,
guarding secrets
those are…they are—
were he to capture one—

Now

· ·

Throwing pebbles
into that pond
As we had in the not so long ago
each yesteryear
like the ripple
disappearing
gentle
still
your fingertips
upon my translucent
wrinkled
memories
alighting
upon our weary
bodies
our lips
muted
&
washed
weathered
echoing
seconds
this
our
now…

The Devil's Pulpit

Somewhere beyond
A glen
Kilkearn
The Devil's Pulpit
Where the sun
Like butter
On hot toast
Melts into the Earth
Lovers
Dance
A tango
Upon the green
Green
Grass
Softly
Deftly
Aligned
Keeping tempo

To the stream's
Rhythm
Passions
Pouring
Out
Like Molasses…

The Ebb

Dawn
Tiptoes
Upon the water
Curling
Barefooted
Toes
Trapping
Waltzing
Foam
Lazily
Through
The ebb
And
Flow
In the now
Night
Comes
Too soon.

Forever Life

it is only when night calls
I awaken to Earth's delights
Scooping up bits of cast-offs
Some ignored…reposing,
though not very well
beneath the well-traveled highways and byways
where only the hallowing winds
and furious blizzards
dare to enter
and rusty metal cans
crackle out the jarring sound of
fire
behold the plumes
dancing out,
recoiling in disgust
their longue dirge
AH! Society's epoch…
and beyond this
Truth and reality
the single events
thus…the vampires
(it would seem) are
mourning what might have been—
and in reality
cast off the lingering shine of that North Star—
Daybreak
Enemy of the state of the forevers
Existing
Existing

The Following

- -

-on the following day
with hell's fury at her back
she reawakened,
swatting away yesterday's fires
as THE PHOENIX
rose
caught her breath—greedily
gulping down saplings
only to release them…
among the cooled grey-white ash
and Mother Earth
with a wink and knowing nod
did welcome all.

My Loves

• •

I love the feel of snowflakes upon my tongue
Wishing I could catch them all
Before
In harmony blanket the earth
Soothing
Comforting
In contentment
Ease away weariness
Too long helplessly watching
Chaos—discord—and some
Righteous indignation
Respite…
While slightly below
Awaits the resurgence…rebirth of crocuses
Lavender
Daffodils
All…but for that winter's thaw
And April's quenching
Once again…life
I love the sound of children's laughter
In innocence and wonderments
Swinging

Tiny legs pumping out in rhythm to the bluebird's tune
I love the feel of my lover's arms
Cradling me forever close…
The beatings of our hearts
One.
I love the sight of butterflies and bumblebees
Waltzing once again…
God's nectar safely
Adoringly
Cherishing
The inexplicable substance only they realize.
I love the tink-tink-tink of an early dawn's rain
Like notes played out
Brahms
Bach
Beethoven
A moonlight sonata
To follow

Soon after, the dried earth
Warmed
Dried
Still
The feel
The sound of gurgle, squish-squish between my toes…
I Love…

The Night Warrior

In this disquieting silence
Stars vying for their moment
Willing the moon
D
  E
    S
      C
        E
          N
            D
Into the surreal
Where wayward imps and their offspring
feast upon the devil's dust
The Night Warrior
In that house so hastily constructed
Upon brimstones and
Fire
Hail…
Oblivion
Where even shadows dare not go,
in sweet repose the brave.
Talking Dante…
No
One would understand
Purgatory
That limbo
Where the outs
Meet
The Ins.
And chaos' tortured mind
Out of hibernation
Gulps down the remains of
The Remains.

My painted Self

i had measured my life

in cups of sugar

and in those moments

filled with days of

hopscotch

hula hoops

tootsie rolls

and ice cream cones

ignored

but…just dancing in the sudden bursts

of summer rains—

Mamma calling

while i so welcoming

of distant rainbows

and the plink-plink-plink

of drops echoing

off the city's this and that

chasing dreams and unicorns—

oh!

and just like that—

time

like vultures feasting upon carcasses in the desert

swooped up my youth

swallowing hard

tearing away the what was—

hopscotch

hula hoops

tootsie rolls

and ice cream cones

too quickly

in gallons

My painted Self

and I'm okay!

The Naked Sky

• •

We have reached the apex
It is comforting
lying curled up in your arms
Your warm breath
Births my soul
That vermilion…
My ocean of love
my monolith
and the slow dance of your heart
my lullaby
Beneath the Naked Sky

Re-awakenings

. . . .

Imperceptible ghosts
(It would appear)
Illuminated by that midnight sky
That those others might not see
Imagine
Envision
Catch and release
—should it be transient—
The same
Yet
different
With their fixed stares
As if heaven had the answer
Voices in their minds
Would shatter the hallowed silence
Chasing…
in a game
Perhaps of throw and catch
M squared
or that
and this
Being Einstein
the curvature of space
the distribution of mass
Energy
with some constants
(Just that)
Accelerated Motion
by chance
or accident
without explanations
No matter

Formulas do not apply
You see
Here it just IS
The All—
Playing
Catch
with that greater purpose
slumbering no longer
The Rip Van Winkles
10 years
20…30
What secrets will be revealed?
Tiptoeing
take hold
So eagerly rising before the sun.
Enveloped in cocoons
temporarily discarded
Arias call
and
they respond
Though eyes still fixed
to heaven
It calls their re-awakening
'Rise'
Calls
Music
They shall respond
for night may fall too quickly
As it always does—

A Hero fallen

• •

There
The remains of the day
His remains
Triangular red, white, and blue
And just beyond
The pulling of seven triggers
Standard number…weapons
Biblical?
Mythical?
Hearts skipping a beat as each
Firing echoes out
Even birds
still unaccustomed
Take flight.
Family and friends
With the remains of memories
'Late again,' mom scolded
And oh…she would welcome that lateness now
Dad wanted one last water fight as they washed that relic
Held together by spit and prayer
A small sip of New Year's Champagne
His friends to 'Auld Lang Syne'…farewell.
A glass or two or more if mom and dad weren't watching…
'Auld Lang Syne.'
That rocket's red glare…
And while 'bombs were bursting midair…'
Sand dunes imploding
Exploding
Turning skies and earth sad red…
Marching on…keep marching on…
'Forever May it wave!
Storming Normandy—

112

And Korea…the forgotten forged
To Vietnam
While Agent Orange was bursting midair
And the innocent could be innocent…
But no one seemed to ask
And the banging of the drum
The troops keep marching in…
Sometimes—
And the remains of the day
The blue with gold trimmed urn
(Mamma had bought as a beautiful piece of art for her curio)
Flat upon a makeshift altar
A pendant dangling in eerie silence
Around its neck…
A Purple Heart—
It does not bleed out
Or shrapnel torn…remains
Marking the weres or might have beens
The Purple Heart!
"…for being wounded or killed in any action against
an enemy of the United States or as a result of an act
of any such enemy or opposing armed forces…'
Don't YOU know!
The Hero Fallen—
…and HIS TRUTH KEEPS MARCHING…on

And the Music Died

••

…all anyone would hear
was the sound of silence

Blahblahblahblah
AC DC
Monitored
Even the leafy sea dragon
Camouflaged in seaweed
Filtered out the
blahblablahblah
White noise
&
Gamma rays…
Mixed with copious verbiage
That reveals nothing
RKO
As far as acronyms go
&
music died

The Waiting

Look for me when darkness eats away the sun
Still in my innocence
Whispering secrets to my friend
The same one who held my hand
When you had to let me go
I'll wait
I'll send you big hugs
& soft kisses
Wiping away those endless tears
Why's
Illusive
Perverse
I'll be waiting.

You! You! You!

∙ ∙

Holding on
At the threshold
It is there
Our eternity
Where there exists no separation
Each feather touch of your fingertips
My skin gives way
And I am consumed
Desire unleashed
That once unsated want
Newly discovered
My treasure trove
Greedily I shall…
You and I
One entity
Fueled and thrust
Scattered
Then
Collected—
You
You
As I close my eyes
Wrapped in the lavender musk
Foam upon the never-ending tide—
Our El Dorado
Beyond the heavens
We are…
We are…
Catching my breath
You! You! You!

The artist

Bring me your heart
I shall forever
Keep it beating
Immortalized upon my canvas
And lovingly
Upon the voids
I shall caress the contours
Of your supple lips
Lingering…
Lingering…
Smoothing out
Those words
That waited patiently
Deeper still
Those chestnut eyes
That peer into my soul
All this…
The artist!

In Contemplation

• •

In contemplation
Never shall I think
Of those hours spent
Your fingers adapted
To that silence
That spoke of sorrow
And a love that would not
Could not…
Take hold
Grow
In contemplation
Sorrow
Separate
Living the dark
And damned
In contemplation
Of moving in reverse
Crazy
Simple
Weaving in circles
Each step
Thought of what if's
Forevers
Left unharvested
In the letting go.

Good Bad Neither Black Nor White

Standing on the edge of a precipice
Watching Crows feeding Doves
Beneath
Blended
Separated
But,
Still
I watch through my unfiltered lenses
Inching closer to that edge
Neither good nor bad
Though the impending storm
Announced by Fog
And hateful thunder
Would have me believe otherwise
And farther yet
Where the woodpecker
Taps away at a fallen branch
While beetles burrow
Through the thinning bark
And Skeletal Blooms
Bask uninterrupted
In the early morning sun
Neither Good
Neither Bad
I
Till the fading of the sun
Hastens my retreat
Forever...
Crows feeding Doves...
Neither Good
Neither Bad.

Saint and Sinner
Anima and Animus

· ·

Close your eyes

Free fall

Juxtaposed Saint and Sinner

Forever intertwined

The music starts

Passion's fury

Saint and Sinner

Respond

In the rhythm of night's calling

Each seductive

Yearning

The Kizomba

Echoes near

In twists, turns

Legs

Hips

Guttural

Collecting

Orgasmic whispers

The just before

Like the sudden cataclysmic eruption

Vesuvius

Krakatoa

Mt. Pelee

Santa Maria

In molten magma

Lava

Ash

Too quickly follow

And in that final release

Anima and Animus!

The Tsunami

Inhaling
My soul does fly
In a multitude of shifts
Where men dare not tread
In oceans deep
Muted rumblings only
A few will hear
When all else slips away
And the only sound
Two hearts
Two minds
As one
Inhaling
Embracing
The final
Tsunami

There—

• •

Are you still there?

Sitting upon your throne

In your magnificent omnipotence

Wondering if gifting free will

Was not a well-planned gift after all—

Rolling that minuscule pebble

In your now

Calloused and ancient

Rheumatoid

Twisted fingers

Trying

With that great strength

To hold onto…

That orb

Cast upon

Black velveteen

Bespectacled golds

Their guide

All with your artist's hands

But now—

That pebble

Your Earth

Their earth

Oh! How simple

To rest it upon your thumb

And flick it ALL away

With that

pointer

Or with one puff

Scatter it to the NEVER was—

Smash it into your upraised palms

And there

earth

and nothing...else—

Are you there?

Maria

● ●

And in that final release, her energy broke free—
A fragmented shell lying still—
She glided upon an ethereal glow—
Of golds-lavender and a color—
Undiscovered—
Unnamed—
Vespers
Echoing
Down the hospice walls—
Joining the group
Gathered there—
arms wide
The welcome home!

Punic Wars

Cruel words

Like shards of glass

Cutting

Away the forgiving

Bits

Of fond memories

I bleed out

In the not so long ago

Where yellow daisies

Knew me well

And chased windmills

My makeshift sword

Like Don Quixote

Punic Wars

Battles

Won and lost

A soldier's valiant

Effort

A Purple Heart

Little solace

In silenced

Whispers

Hitches

A final ascent

Upon that shadowed stairway

Juxtaposed

Just beyond

Tangible

Earth

And

Angel fantasies

Flannel

Lying here
Wishing
Passions
Rebirth
The old
Flannel shirt
You wore
While nursing
Seedlings
On late spring evenings
Later
Nature's tendrils
Basking in the sun
&
In grieving eternity
A flannel comforter
Holding fast
Onto our spent ecstasy
I forever
Scream
For you

Five Lines

• •

Following the path where shadows lead
Catching monarchs
Only to release them
Once again
To follow their own transient shadows—

Beneath the Glen

Somewhere beyond
A glen
Kilkearn
The Devil's Pulpit
Where the sun
Like butter
On hot toast
Melts into the Earth
Lovers
Dance
A tango
Upon the green
Green
Grass
Softly
Deftly
Aligned
Keeping tempo
To the stream's
Rhythm
Passions
Pouring
Out
Like Molasses.

1

Cherry wine kisses
Scarlet
Raindrops
Caressing
Quenching
My thirst
Maddening
My body
Pink sand under your touch
Rising
Falling
Catch me
Wanting forever
I weep
In passions
Flames
You catch my tears
A lover's murmur
2
THEN
1

Barkeep

Pretzel crumbs

Like gnats

Caught in a spiderweb

He tethered

On the barstool

Gray smoke

Greet dull lights

From his L&Ms

As he

Taps

With calloused

Fingers

his life's

Regrets

Four Roses

Beer chasers

The World

Stops

No one notices

Cares

"Fill 'er up!"

Knocks it back

&
chases it!

Stones Like Feathers

Skipping Stones
Watching
Dancing ripples
Waltzing
Effortlessly
Catching
The joyous
Sunlight
Crystalline
Stars
Bouncing
In unison
Upon the water
Silence
But for the Summer
Dove
Cooing
In approval
Respite—
Basking
under the sun's umbrella—
Sipping orange blossom tea!

Silage

· ·

It was there
Then
Now
Holding on
Letting go
A memory
Prances in
On a butterfly's
Wings
A magnolia fully bloomed
Your breaths
My own
Erotic
Filling
Nooks
My senses
Scattered
That magical potion
mind
Bursting
Wanting
Touch
Me
Inhale
Musky
Silage
Erotic
The blue moon
Calls

Forever the innocent

Child
Of the
oh so
too quickly gone—
Open Meadows
Concrete slabs
Crushing
Supplanting
Dandelion
Wishes
Only I heard
Beneath
An earth
Where
Flowers
Still
DO
BLOOM
Listen
They know you by name
Seedlings
Lying in fretful
Slumber
Peeking
Thru
Lines
&
Cracks—

Lips

· ·

Abandoned senses
falling into
his eyes
a mirror
my own
Rising desire
erotic
musk
mingling
in ocean's ebb and tide
salty
drenched
yearning
blood boiling
made it all
So clear
Reaching
that point
heat
my mind
This is my forever
Wanting him to inhale my soul.

Quill

●●

To papyrus
Ancient memories
My mind
A weaver of magic
Spells
Poet
Dipping my weathered quill
Into my fountain
Of sadness
Spilling out
With ease
A few words
Mingling with
Dried tears
Ignorant fool
It's only when sadness
Is penned—
A tear
Dries.

Blink

• •

Meeting the sun—
Above
Cement
Steel
Screeching
Brakes
Concrete
Graves
But
For
A brave dandelion
Calling
Me
Make a wish
Pleading
stay
Sad
I could not
Stop
midflight
Torn
In a nanosecond
Blink
Disappears
And I
In this realm
Of what now?
Dared not
Look
Back.

Daddy's flower

One final
Moment
Holding your hand
Willing you
2NEVER
Let go
Hazel eyes
Blankly staring
At no
One
Just you
And
I
A comfortable
Silence
A WAKE
Funeral
Procession

A fleeting memory
Of a time
Not too long ago
When—
You called me
"A small flower by my side."

Wickedly

· ·

Holding you close
Your heart
Beating
A tender ballad
Quivering
With anticipation
Time
Frozen
In
Your harmony
A perfect duet
Whispering
Ethereal
Hymns
Into my waiting
Soul
Quenching
My parched lips
Far too long
Had I
Waited
Under
That desert
Sun!

Mamma said—

· ·

"Always act like a lady!"
While dad guzzled down the last of his Roses with the Facades
And
Veneers-lackluster-stained with yesteryears' remnants
in silence—
Wearing $1 sandals & dumpster clothing—
"Act like a lady!"
gently polished
Staged—
Shakespearean tragedy
Last call!

144

Thirst

....

Smother my words
With your lips
Tongue
Caressing
Each poetic
Rhythm
Formed
Take me
With you
Hell's FIRE
Eager tendrils
Surrendering
To gentle
Fingers
Moist
Skimming
Circular
Patterns
On hand-blown
Crystal
Quench
My thirst
ecstasy
Pales
The summer sun
Come!

Sadness Implodes

Holding on
Letting go
Torn between
Then
Now
Later
Transparent
Threadbare
Glint
Of hope
My mind
Imploding
Half truths
And Never
Land
Fragments
Scattered
Through a satiated
Miasma
Were my soul
To
Follow
I would
Not
Weep
For it is there
My spirit
Explodes
Love's
Rebirth!

Alzheimer's

Will you be here
When winter's shadows
Waltz down
On angels' wings
Hold my hand
Call my name
Tell me yours
As my memory
Like a desert oasis
Disappears
When I blink?
Kiss me gently
Each time
Today
Like the first time
Gather
My memories
Gift them
One by
One
When
Winter—
Angels—

A Waltz Upon the Horizon

Raindrop kisses
A hint of honey
Sticky sweet
Remnants
First
Last
Lingering forever
In the in between
Falling
Gliding
Rising
Caught
In the soulful
Images
Of your gold rimmed
Emerald eyes
Side-by-side
Knowing
Ambers
dawn
Upon the horizon
A ballet
Today
Today…

The Illuminations

• •

Shadows
Fading
Falling
Through
Oblivion
Where chaos
Betrayal
Pain
Prisoners
All
Beneath
An illuminating
Star
Fire
Long ago
The yesterdays
Ashes
Churning
A midnight's vesper
Illuminated
Transient
Hollows
Out
The memories
And
Weeping
Covers
ALL
With
Diphylleia!

Sundays

· ·

In the tenderness
Of the night

I catch your warmth
Cuddling

Close for it fills
Me so

Rhythmic
Patterns

Circling
Rediscovering

Paths
Memories

Erotically
Provoking

Time
Etched upon

Approving moonbeams
Feel
Me
Fill
Me

While envious
Stars
Wish—

From somewhere

Within the constraints
Of my beating heart
Droplets
Crimson
Gathered
In an effortless
Dance
The stark white
Paper
Their floor
Whimsical
Romantic
Silly
Erotic
My mind
Dizzy
Intoxicating
Revealing
Me
YES
But
That is not
ALL
I AM!

Bottled Storms

I watched as his head tilted back,
The final drop of his liquid gold a memory.
The empty bottle sat silently glaring up into his foggy eyes,
And as the angry, bellowing of a winter's blizzard knocked at the
    windowpanes,
I wondered when yet another storm would end.

Twilight Begins

Hugging your pillow ever so tightly
For my longing of you
Your warm breath
Against my nape
A feathery touch
Caressing me to sleep
Collecting shooting stars
Remembering wishes
Floating beyond reach
Where your love waits
In twilight kisses
And a comforting embrace

Sloth Summer Days

∙∙∙

Retreating
Caramel
Apple
Crisps
Pie
Fritters
Pumpkin
Spice
Cozy
Campfire
Nights
Wrapped
Toasty
Warm
Watching
Amber
Sparks
Dancing
In your eyes…

Demon Madness

Bring me to madness
A solitary flick of your finger
Arousing
Sensual
I want your smell
The taste of you
Take me to hell
Engulfed
Penetrating
Ecstasy
Even for tonight
Master
My desire
Explore
Seek out
Smother
My hunger
Demon
My body burns
Fueled
Your breath
Madness!

TOO!

As a child
Living in fear
Dad's always drunk
Mom's happy now
Manic soon
&

At night
Dreams—

I flew above the city
Where street lights
Cast shadows upon
The hungry
Restless in their
Cardboard houses
And wondered
If they too
Dreamed
Of having wings like a bird—

Autumn's Dance

There's something
Quite sensual
Watching
Autumnal
Leaves
Caressing
The wind
A slow dance
Amber
Orange
Red
Eroticism
Gooey
Caramel Apples
Pumpkin spice
Lingering
Long after
Hungry
Kisses
Arcadia
Cocoa hue
Just after
Twilight
Snuggling
Under
Our
Worn plaid
Blanket.

Time Too Quickly—

The grandfather's clock
Remains
Sadly
Silenced
Tick-tick-tock
Ding-ding-ding
A fleeting memory
When time was measured
Through the opening
Of an eye dropper
Tick-tick-tock
Ding-ding-ding
Days when
Children
Ran screeching
Down the spiral
Case
disappeared
Into
Adulthood—

Enough

· ·

Today I shall
Discard
That relic
I once called
Home
Soul
Restrained
Contained
Imprisoned
Interred
Today
Today
Immortal
Release
Manumit
You have
Starved me long
Enough
Enough
Subdued
Subjugated
Questioned
I did not inhabit
Your body
You bound mine
A gift
Unopened
Enough.

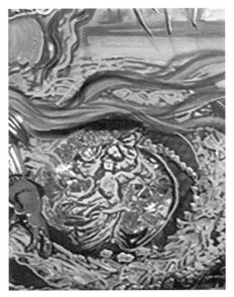
(Chris W Tutty)

Screeching Shadows

He headed to his
Old friend
At the far corner
Of the bar
The cracked leather
Moaned
As he sat
Watching
Shadows
Apparitions
Coming
Going
Four down
Bourbon
The lost soul
Moniker
His fingers
Tap
Tapping
Minutes
Of his existence.

The Lullaby

Pianista
Cords
Tethered
Black
White
Sitting
Stroking
An infant's touch
Ninnanna
Lullaby
Releasing
Rhythmic oeuvre
Of colors
Disquiet
Refrain
Pianista
Forte
Adagio
Sonance
A euphony
Where an
Infant dreams
Tintamarre
Dolcemente
Dreaming
The colorful
Berceuse!

A Time...

A time of turtlenecks
Love beads
Moonlights
Incense
Burning in every
Corner
Store
Pot smoking hippies
On their
Rotary
Phones
White doves
Peace signs
James Dean
Elvis
Stones
Beatlemania
Woodstock
Where have all the flowers gone?
Vietnam
I'm afraid
The dove has flown!

Ferwech

Away from turbulent
Places
Gather me up
Calm
Sanctuary
Where
Strength
Weaves
Indestructible
Webs
Fortitude
It is
There
Just beyond
Those
Turbulent
Demons
Where white
Trumpet
Lilies
Grow
And the true
Elysian
Sky
Exists!

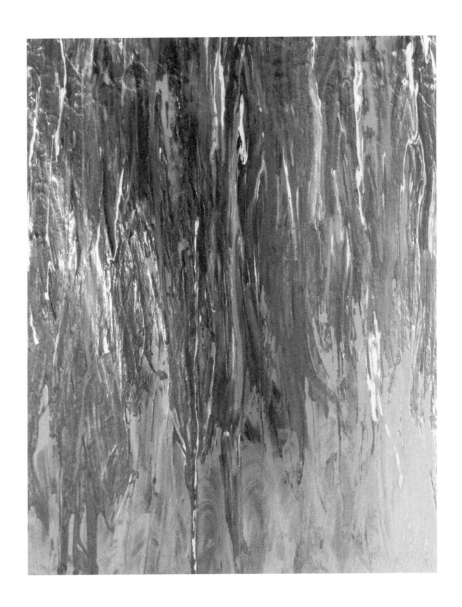

Were I

· ·

A hummingbird
Lavender
Blue
Yellow
Green
My music
From my theremin
Strings
And the sound
Of my own heart
Keeping
Tempo
To the mystic
Flapping of my wings
Feeding on nectar
Stunt
Flying
An invisible plane
A roller coaster
My theremin
And
I
Poem—

Cherry wine

On his fingertips
Tracing
Erotic
Circles
Along the contours
Of my lips
My body followed
Greedily
His lips
Wine
Bodies
Happily
Fantastically
Drunk
A slow dance
Of yearning
Limbo
Between
Nothing
And
No one
Suspended
Waiting's
Breathless…

Jamais

· ·

Arms wide
Open
Fill me
Take me
To the sun's
Birthplace
Drench
My soul
With hues
Of gold
Embrace
Me
Fully
Gently
Hold me
There
And never
Let me go!

J.S. Frankel was born in Toronto, Canada and grew up there, receiving his tertiary education from the University of Toronto and graduating with a double major in English Literature and Political Science. After working at Gray Coach Lines for a grand total of three years, he came to Japan at the age of twenty-six and has been there ever since, teaching English to all who enter his hallowed school of learning.

In 1997, he married Akiko Koike. He, his wife and his two children, Kai and Ray, currently reside in Osaka. His hobbies include weight training, watching movies when his writing schedule allows, and listening to various kinds of music.

His novels, all for the YA set, include the Catnip series, Master Fantastic, Moonlighters, What The Gods Allow, and The Oddities, all courtesy of Extasy Books dot com. Future projects for Extasy include Hoppers, Twisted, and Sideshow, among others. He is also the author of The Menagerie and The Nightmare Crew trilogy, all courtesy of Finch Books.

Link: (Amazon) https://www.amazon.com/J-S-Frankel/e/
B004XUUTB8/ref=dp_byline_cont_pop_ebooks_1
(Extasy Books) https://www.extasybooks.com/j.s.-frankel

Paul Simeone is a pianist/vocalist/composer who has been making music since he was a child. From his days playing the accordion at age six, to his current role as a solo and group performer, he's always held the gift of music in a prominent place of his life. Before recently retiring, he was the choral director for thirty-five years at Ridgefield Park Junior/Senior High School in New Jersey. He's performed in numerous venues over the years, playing various styles of music (pop, R&B, Broadway, jazz, etc.) and is still performing live today.

He has recently started working with Anna Casamento Arrigo on providing music for her poetry, namely "Ain't Got No Time" from the book, "Changeling." "Closer," and "Once Upon A Fairytale," are found on the pages of her sixth collection of poems entitled "Anima" ("Closer" can currently be found on SoundCloud). Most recently, they have composed two additional songs, included in this collection ("Butterflies and Bumblebees" which is a profoundly moving piece, and "The Perfect Distance," that focuses on Domestic Violence Awareness)! Of all the aspects of making music he has experienced throughout his life, composing and recording his own compositions is still his favorite activity. Paul and his wife Lori are currently spending their semi-retirement years living happily ever after in New Jersey...

More of Paul Simeone's music is available on SoundCloud, Spotify, Apple Music, Amazon Music Unlimited, YouTube Music, Pandora Radio, iHeart Radio, Tidal and Deezer.

Anna Casamento Arrigo was born in Sorrentini, Sicily, and came to America with her family to settle in New Jersey many years ago. Tragedy struck when she suffered a life-altering stroke. Conventional therapy helped, but writing proved to be the greatest therapy of all when she turned to creating poetry to express her innermost thoughts and fears and desires. Music also provided inspiration, and after combining aspects of music, prose, and classical literature, she devised her own style of writing, something intensely personal, almost visionary. Prior to her stroke, Mrs. Casamento Arrigo taught many inner city students, inspiring them to do better. Children need inspiration, and once they find it in themselves, they are capable of anything. That is her motto, and she has used to pass on her knowledge to her five children and her twelve grandchildren. For her, learning is not enough. Imparting that knowledge to others unselfishly remains her focus on life. She has penned numerous books in a variety of genres including her memoir, a romance novel, several collections of poetry, this is her seventh, as well as several children's books. She does not want to be tied to any specific genre and wishes to explore the limits of each genre she chooses at any given time.
In terms of her personal recovery, Mrs. Casamento Arrigo continues to strive to regain what has been lost. Writing provides that spark of creativity, one that she has used to create more children's books as well as a series of short stories plus another memoir.

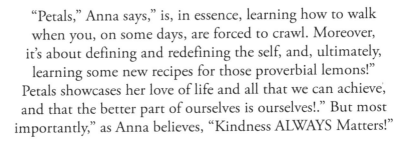

"Petals," Anna says," is, in essence, learning how to walk when you, on some days, are forced to crawl. Moreover, it's about defining and redefining the self, and, ultimately, learning some new recipes for those proverbial lemons!" Petals showcases her love of life and all that we can achieve, and that the better part of ourselves is ourselves!." But most importantly," as Anna believes, "Kindness ALWAYS Matters!"

Moonstruck Cover Design & Photography Emma Rider for Petals.

Lightning Source UK Ltd.
Milton Keynes UK
UKHW050841260223
417579UK00013B/82